DECO TECH

GEOMETRIC COLORING BOOK

JOHN WIK

DOVER PUBLICATIONS, INC. • MINEOLA, NEW YORK

GREEN EDITION ®

At Dover Publications we're committed to producing books in an earth-friendly manner and to helping our customers make greener choices.

Manufacturing books in the United States ensures compliance with strict environmental laws and eliminates the need for international freight shipping, a major contributor to global air pollution. And printing on recycled paper helps minimize our consumption of trees, water and fossil fuels.

The text of this book was printed on paper made with 50% post-consumer waste and the cover was printed on paper made with 10% post-consumer waste. At Dover, we use Environmental Paper Network's Paper Calculator to measure the benefits of these choices, including: the number of trees saved, gallons of water conserved, as well as air emissions and solid waste eliminated.

Courier Corporation, the manufacturer of this book, owns the Green Edition Trademark.

Please visit the product page for *Deco Tech: Geometric Coloring Book* at www.doverpublications.com to see a detailed account of the environmental savings we've achieved over the life of this book.

NOTE

The thirty black-and-white illustrations in this coloring book provide an array of interesting designs—all of them utilizing the many possibilities of geometric shapes! The exciting combination of circles, squares, and triangles amongst a countless number of creative lines, angles, and curves creates an entertaining challenge that will please colorists of all ages. Use colored pencils, markers, paints, or other media, and bring these distinctive designs to life!

Copyright

Copyright © 2010 by Dover Publications, Inc.
All rights reserved.

Bibliographical Note

Deco Tech: Geometric Coloring Book is a new work, first published by Dover Publications, Inc., in 2010.

International Standard Book Number

ISBN-13: 978-0-486-47546-2
ISBN-10: 0-486-47546-8

Manufactured in the United States by Courier Corporation
47546805
www.doverpublications.com

1

3

11

14

16

17

18

19